BEYOND GENDER BINARIES

THE HISTORY OF TRANS, INTERSEX, AND THIRD-GENDER INDIVIDUALS

THE HISTORY OF THE LGBTQ+ RIGHTS MOVEMENT™

BEYOND GENDER BINARIES

THE HISTORY OF TRANS, INTERSEX, AND THIRD-GENDER INDIVIDUALS

RITA SANTOS

Rosen
YA
New York

To my baby sister, Kiera

Published in 2019 by The Rosen Publishing Group, Inc.
29 East 21st Street, New York, NY 10010

Library of Congress Cataloging-in-Publication Data

Names: Santos, Rita, 1985– author.
Title: Beyond gender binaries : the history of trans, intersex, and third-gender individuals / Rita Santos.
Description: New York : Rosen Publishing, 2019. | Series: The history of the LGBTQ+ rights movement | Includes bibliographical references and index. | Audience: Grades 7–12.
Identifiers: LCCN 2017019683 | ISBN 9781538381267 (library bound) | ISBN 9781508183075 (pbk.)
Subjects: LCSH: Transgender people—History—Juvenile literature. | Intersex people—History—Juvenile literature. | Sexual minorities—History—Juvenile literature.
Classification: LCC HQ73 .S26 2018 | DDC 306.76/8—dc23
LC record available at https://lccn.loc.gov/2017019683

Manufactured in the United States of America

On the cover: Shown here are Christine Jorgensen (*top*), who became well known after her gender affirmation surgery was announced in 1952, and actress Laverne Cox (*bottom*).

CONTENTS

INTRODUCTION

Some people use the terms "sex" and "gender" interchangeably, but they refer to two different things. In biology, "sex" refers to the physical being of a person. The most common types of bodies have either male or female reproductive systems, so some would take this to mean that one's sex must fit one of the binary categories. However, some people are intersex and have reproductive systems that don't fit what is typically categorized as male or female, so these people don't fit into the male/female binary in a biological sense.

Gender refers to how we feel about ourselves on a mental level. Binary thinking suggests that there are only two genders: male and female. However, human psychology is much more complicated than this either/or scenario suggests. Much investigation has led scientists to believe that gender is really more of a spectrum. People can fall anywhere along this spectrum at or in between male and female psychological identities, or they may feel that their identity doesn't fit into a spectrum that relies on feminine or masculine characterizations.

To complicate matters further, signs of gender are based on culture, not biology. While people signify gender with their hairstyles or clothes, those signals come from the meaning society places on those things, and those interpretations change all the time. This signaling is called gender presentation, and for many people, presentation is a way of showing gender identity.

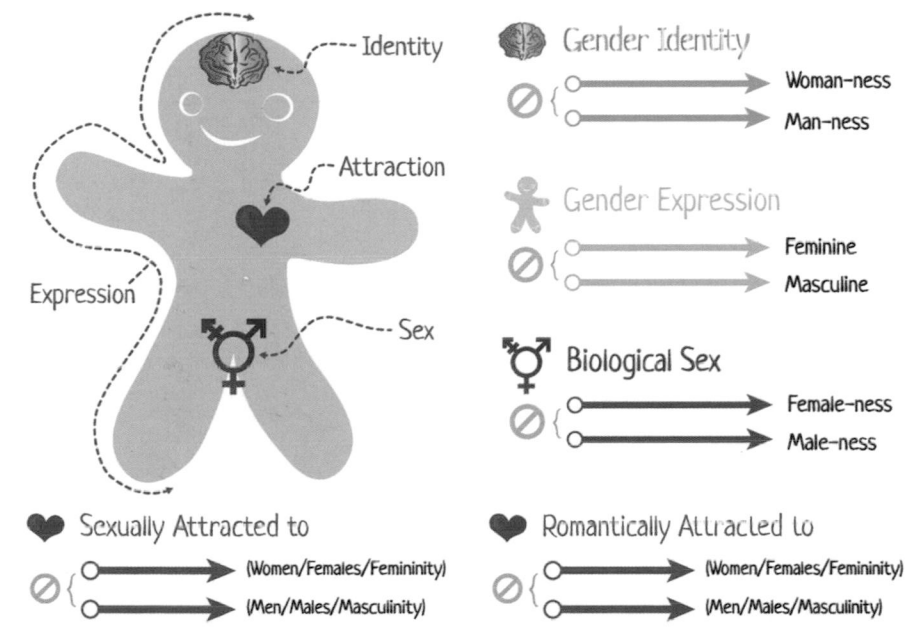

The Genderbread Person v3.3 by its pronounced METROsexual.com

Identity

Attraction

Expression

Sex

Gender Identity
⊘ { Woman-ness
Man-ness

Gender Expression
⊘ { Feminine
Masculine

Biological Sex
⊘ { Female-ness
Male-ness

❤ Sexually Attracted to
⊘ { (Women/Females/Femininity)
(Men/Males/Masculinity)

❤ Romantically Attracted to
⊘ { (Women/Females/Femininity)
(Men/Males/Masculinity)

This visual representation of sexual and gendered identities represents the various gendered parts of a person's identity. But it doesn't account for nonbinary people.

But not everyone attempts to convey gender identity through clothing. Some people may prefer to wear traditionally feminine clothes although they identify as a male or a genderless individual. These are gender-nonconforming or nonbinary actions because they present gender that doesn't match society's expectations. Think of clothing like a uniform: wearing a lab coat and a stethoscope doesn't give a person a deep knowledge of medicine, but it can alert other people that this person has received special training that can be useful in certain situations. In the same way, clothes do not give the wearer a gender, but they can tell others how the wearer relates to gender.

For cisgender people, their sex matches their gender. Transgender, or trans, people are aware that some aspect of their gender, gender presentation, and/or sex does not match. Some trans people, sometimes referred to as transsexual, opt to have gender affirmation surgery. Other transgender people don't feel the need or want to have gender affirmation surgery.

Many cultures around the globe have always had nonbinary views of gender. They have approached this phenomenon in positive or negative ways, and these attitudes have produced many historically significant moments. However, separating the history of transgender and nonbinary people from that of gay people isn't always easy. It was only recently that terms to describe the transgender experience came into existence and came to be widely used. It was often the case that transgender people were incorrectly labeled as being homosexual—but even that word wasn't introduced until the late nineteenth century.

The lack of appropriate labeling does not erase the historical examples of nonbinary individuals—it only indicates that anthropologists need to know what to look for. In American history, for example, there are several documented cases of women who presented as male to fight in the Civil War and who then continued to do so after the war ended. The clearly defined gender roles of post–Civil War America allow anthropologists to confidently theorize that some of these women were actually transgender men. But for cultures and historical periods in which genders were less clearly defined, finding those who did not fit into standards of gender or sex normativity can be harder.

CHAPTER ONE

BRAZIL: A LAND OF CONTRADICTIONS

In the sixteenth century, Portugal colonized the many indigenous tribes that make up what is now known as Brazil. The Portuguese sent almost four million enslaved Africans to Brazil to work on sugarcane plantations between the seventeenth and eighteenth centuries. These enslaved people, who would eventually win their freedom, brought their own culture and traditions with them. The intermixing of the indigenous population, the Portuguese, and the Africans created a mixed ethnicity known as the Pardo. The size and ethnic diversity of the country mean that representations of gender change not only between geographic areas, but also between groups. While some areas of the country are accepting of third-gender individuals, many are not.

TRAVESTIS IN BRAZILIAN CULTURE

Gender roles are strictly enforced in Brazil. An important part of gender politics in Brazil stems from its colonial caste system, the means of controlling the enslaved population, plantation overseers, and even free families. This system was established during colonial slavery, which took place from the sixteenth century until the late nineteenth century, but it contributed to the rigidity of gender in Brazilian society long after slavery was abolished.

The male and female genders were seen and treated as opposites. It wasn't just that their physical appearance separated the two genders; men and women were at odds with one another in every way possible. Proper masculine behavior was considered to be very aggressive and dominating, while women were expected to be passove and submissive.

Because genders were treated as opposites, one gender had to dominate. Part of being a man meant having power over women and maintaining that power. If a man was thought of as lacking control over women, he would be perceived as weak or not manly enough. Similarly, a woman who defied a man's attempts to subdue her would not be considered feminine.

Gender-nonconforming people face a similar type of environment. In Brazil, they are often called *travesti*. It's a term that used to be strictly derogatory, but many in the South American LGBTQ+ community are trying to reclaim the word.

"Travesti" is a term that means different things to different people. To some, travesti are transgender women, and to others, they are nonbinary. Effeminate homosexual men, for

A travesti poses for the camera during Brazil's Gay Pride Parade in 2014. The parade serves as a celebration of the LGBTQ+ community.

example, are sometimes considered to be travesti because they do not fit the culture's view of what it is to be a man. However, a masculine homosexual man is not considered to be a travesti because he still adheres to gender norms of aggressive masculinity.

Travesti are not men but are also not controlled by men. People who are used to strict gender norms might be confused by someone who, in their eyes, "chooses" to give up their superior role in society by identifying as a travesti instead of as a man. People who don't conform to gender norms cause others in their society to question how valid those norms are. This kind of questioning can make people feel uncomfortable and threatened.

THE MOST BEAUTIFUL WOMAN IN BRAZIL

Roberta Close, assigned male at birth, knew she was different. At eighteen years old, she arrived for her military conscription wearing a dress. By then, she had already secretly begun hormone therapy. It's unclear if the Brazilian military knew that, but she was excused from service.

But that wouldn't be her only rejection. Close's family disowned her when they found out that she was a transgender woman.

Close managed to start a modeling career. Although her legal surname was Moreira, everyone knew her as Roberta Close. Close also had a short film and television career as an actress, but her main passion was modeling.

In fact, she was quite popular on the runway and off. At twenty, she won the Miss Gay Brazil beauty pageant. In 1989, following gender affirmation surgery in London, she was featured in a popular Brazilian men's magazine called *Sexy*. Readers voted her the "most beautiful woman in Brazil." She was even featured in *Vogue*.

(continued on the next page)

The Brazilian Supreme Court is located in Brasília. Some of Roberta Close's greatest victories were achieved there.

(continued from the previous page)

In 1997, the Brazilian Supreme Court refused to allow Close to change her gender on her birth certificate and other identifying documents. Still, Close refused to give up. In 2005, the Brazilian court finally recognized Close's true gender and issued her a new birth certificate. Later in life, Close learned from a genetic test that she was intersex.

GENDER PERFORMANCE AND DANGER

Brazilians pride themselves on outward beauty and appearance. Similarly, travestis often become interested in their appearance. The phrase *solta plumas*, or "releasing feathers," refers to someone who is accepting their travesti status and becoming more outwardly feminine.

Many people, travestis and cisgender women alike, choose to have plastic surgery in order to better meet the Brazilian standard of beauty. Some travestis choose to undergo hormone therapy as children before they enter puberty. However, it's uncommon for travestis to choose to have any gender-related surgery, especially for those who do not view themselves as women. They often only desire to act in traditionally feminine ways.

There is also a degree of external influence involved in the decision to outwardly change one's appearance. Fitting in well with gendered beauty standards in Brazil often meets with less street harassment. However, any beauty standard that someone must submit to in order to avoid unwanted attention is repressive and unhealthy.

In fact, in most areas of the world, gender-nonconforming people face intolerance and violence. Brazil has one of the world's highest violent crime rates. Violence against travestis, in particular, is also common there. The travesti community is one of the most marginalized and stigmatized groups in Brazilian society. In some

LGBTQ+ activists and their allies in Rio de Janeiro march in solidarity with the victims of the Pulse nightclub shooting, a mass shooting that occurred in Orlando, Florida, in 2016.

areas, the threat of violence is so high that many travestis refuse to leave their homes. Police brutality against travestis is also common, and crimes against queer people are usually not investigated.

In February 2017, a cell phone video of several people beating Dandara dos Santos, a transgender woman, appeared on YouTube. She was later shot in the head. While the video did not capture the moment of dos Santos's murder, police were able to use it to arrest five of the men involved in her torture and murder.

The video brought attention to the incredibly high murder rate of travestis in Brazil. Christian religious groups have been successful in blocking antidiscrimination laws in Brazil for many years, but activists are hopeful that the outpouring of sympathy for dos Santos will finally help the laws get passed. Antidiscrimination laws are a great first step in the fight toward keeping everyone safe.

THE CONTRADICTIONS OF CARNIVAL

Brazil, like much of Latin America, is primarily a Catholic country. Every year before Lent, Catholics around the world celebrate carnival, a festival that is partially meant to celebrate the seasonal change from winter to spring but also one in which the normal social order is upended.

However, carnival wasn't always associated with Catholicism. It began as a widespread European pagan celebration from ancient times that would

TRANS DAY OF REMEMBRANCE

The violence that gender-nonconforming people face is not unique to Brazil. Unfortunately, this experience is common in other countries as well. In 2015, *Time* magazine revealed that 80 percent of transgender Americans report experiencing harassment in school.

In 1998, a group of activists decided to memorialize all the transgender and gender-nonconforming people who were killed over the span of a year. On November 20, 1999, the first Transgender Day of Remembrance was held in San Francisco. The event occurs in cities all over America each year. In 2016, the names of several transgender women of color were read at this event. The event is meant not only to honor those whose lives were lost to intolerance and bigotry, but also to highlight how little law enforcement does in these cases.

drive out the winter. The Catholic Church failed on numerous occasions to ban carnival festivities, so it decided to include them under the guise of Christianity instead. When brought to Latin America during the conquest, it was limited geographically to urban areas, while being inclusive of people from all walks of life, including citizens, the enslaved, and women.

The street parties and parades are the largest celebration in Brazil and usually last a week.

Elaborately decorated costumes and parade floats are staples of carnival. So, too, are travestis. While the wider Brazilian public is often hostile toward travestis, Brazilians celebrate them during carnival. This seasonal attitude change toward travestis is one of the largest contradictions in Brazilian culture. Another contradiction is that while travestis face persecution in the streets, the country also has one of the largest populations of transgender models.

CHAPTER TWO

NATIVE AMERICANS GO FROM BERDACHE TO TWO-SPIRIT

M any Native American tribes had much less rigid gender rules than the Europeans who documented their culture. Therefore, Europeans' view of gender affected their descriptions of tribal life. Tribes viewed themselves differently, so one must take into account who produced the records of Native American culture.

To Europeans, who had very strict rules about which gender wore which clothing, it was strange to encounter tribes who lacked such distinctions in fashion in relation to gender.

It is also important to acknowledge that while many similarities exist between certain tribes, especially those in the same geographic region, every tribe was and is different. However, there were some common presentations of nonbinary people in Native American tribes, and these customs remained intact, to a certain extent, after colonial exposure.

European colonists learned about very different concepts of gender when they interacted with Native American tribes. These concepts helped shape the colonial view that Native Americans were uncivilized.

NATIVE AMERICAN GENDERS

Thirteen thousand years ago, at around 11000 BCE, the first people arrived in America. Between then and the arrival of European colonizers in the fifteenth and sixteenth centuries CE, they developed many aspects of their cultures that led their people to spiritual and physiological health and happiness. Included in this cultural umbrella was a liberal approach to gender identity, hinging on transgender inclusion.

The French used the term *berdache* to refer to Native Americans who were not classified as men or as women. "Berdache" was a term used to refer to younger partners in male homosexual relationships. However,

We'wha, a two-spirit person, poses for this 1871 photo in the traditionally feminine clothing of the Zuni tribe.

the term derives from an Arabic word meaning "male prostitute," so Native Americans were not pleased with being labeled as such. In an attempt to escape the inherent stigma of the term, Native Americans popularized the term "two-spirit" as a replacement for "berdache" in the 1990s.

There is no unified agreement among Native American tribes concerning what or who is two-spirit. They may be the queer men whom the French encountered. However, women often also hold two-spirit identities. Some married other women, and some fulfilled the role of men. Also, many tribes with binary understandings of gender still accepted that one's physical body did not always match their gender.

While some tribes did have binary views of gender, others recognized up to four genders. For tribes that recognized multiple genders, they were often described as feminine female, masculine female, feminine male, and masculine male. Other tribes considered those whose physical sex did not match their gender presentation to be a third gender unto itself. Each tribe had its own terms for these categories and rules that defined them.

GENDER AS SECULAR AND RELIGIOUS OCCUPATION

Clothing, especially ceremonial clothing, could signify gender. But in many tribes, what defined someone as being third gender was their gravitation toward roles and occupations held by the other gender.

OSH-TISCH

The Crow referred to trans women as *bade*, and they were an accepted part of the community.

Osh-Tisch, a bade, was such a fierce Crow warrior that her name translates to "Finds Them and Kills Them." Osh-Tisch had been made famous in her tribe by her participation in the Battle of the Rosebud.

In the late 1890s, however, American agents forced the bade, including Osh-Tisch, to cut their hair in masculine styles and dress as men. War Chief Joseph Medicine Crow said, "It was a tragedy, trying to change them." This interference by white settlers forced the bade out of the Crow culture. Osh-Tisch would be one of the last.

In this 1887 photograph, settlers hold members of the Crow tribe as prisoners despite the fact that the tribe was aligned with the settlers.

This gravitation would usually begin in childhood. Some tribes even had a ceremony that typically took place during puberty to allow the person to officially assume a different gender in the eyes of the tribe.

In some tribes, the crafts made by transgender women or third-gender people were seen as being of a higher quality. Trans men were said to be fiercer warriors. Some tribes even thought trans women made better wives. In some tribes, gender-nonconforming people were allowed to perform both male and female jobs, allowing these people to become very wealthy. However, some tribes allowed traditionally female or male occupations to be performed by the other gender without acknowledging that the person was pf a third or fourth gender. This was true even of tribes that had multiple genders.

In the majority of Native American tribes, spiritual power and gender variations went hand in hand. Visions or dreams were common ways to signify that someone was of a different gender. These dreams often involved someone being handed tools of the opposite gender by a deity. Sometimes a pregnant woman's dreams would be seen as a sign that her child would be a third- or fourth-gender person.

Many tribes ascribed holy or sacred positions to gender-nonconforming people. Early European colonists generally did not understand the significance of these spiritual roles within the tribes. When they wrote about third- or fourth-gender people, they would focus more on the person's clothing than their spiritual role. While some tribes did exclude gender-nonconforming people from certain rituals or sacred roles, it was more common for their status to be elevated.

COLONIZATION CHANGES NATIVES' VIEWS ON GENDER

The records of early sailors are an important resource when studying ancient cultures, but it's important to be critical of such records. These unwitting historians didn't always understand the people they were interacting with and sometimes made the wrong assumptions. Further, the language barriers between European sailors and Native Americans limited their ability to understand each other. For example, Christianity in the early 1900s didn't distinguish between sex and gender. The result was that gender-nonconforming behavior was often considered to be the same thing as being homosexual. Christians usually thought of this behavior as a sin. Missionaries, in particular, made it their goal to end the "sinful" practices they saw around them, believing they were spiritually helping people.

Ever since European colonizers first arrived in North America in 1492, they began imposing their beliefs on non-European people. The Spanish Catholic colonizers who believed homosexuality

ALYHA CEREMONY

In the Mohave tribe, trans women were referred to as *alyha*. When a child who was assumed to be a boy at birth was observed to gravitate toward feminine activities instead of masculine ones around the age of ten or eleven, it was taken as a sign of being an alyha. Initially, the child would be discouraged from these activities.

If the child persisted, however, there would be a transition ceremony. The ceremony would be a surprise for the child and serve as a test to determine whether the child identified as a boy or a girl. The ceremony was also a way to alert the tribe of the child's transition into female socialization.

During the ceremony, the tribe would sing songs. If the child joined the women by dancing the woman's dance, the child would be bathed in the river and then her transition was considered permanent. She would be given a new female name and would no longer answer to her former masculine name. She would also be gifted female clothing during the ceremony. Alyha were sought after as wives because the tribe considered them to be very hard workers.

was a sin were baffled and, at times, disgusted by behavior that they encountered in indigenous tribes. The Spaniards encountered not only Native American men who had sex with other men but also ones who took on female roles in their tribe.

They soon attempted to convert Native Americans so as to fit their own standards. These so-called civilizing techniques manifested in a systemic attempt to erase the culture, history, and in many cases, language of Native American tribes; this was in conjunction with taking over the lands of indigenous peoples in the following decades and centuries.

After gaining dominance over Native Americans, the United States and Canada would often take Native American children from their homes and force them into boarding schools. These were very abusive. The children who lived there were often forbidden from behaving in any way that was reminiscent of their culture, including speaking their native language. If the children disobeyed, they faced corporal punishment and other harsh treatments for any minor violation. Ultimately, these actions by American and Canadian authorities isolated thousands of children from their culture in order to assimilate them to one that would be hostile and discriminatory.

As European views of gender and sexuality began to take hold in Native American culture, many tribes began to turn away from their queer communities. Christian missionaries pushing

This photograph from 1901 is of a music class in Carlisle, Pennsylvania. Settlers used schools like the Carlisle Indian School to abuse Native American students and strip them of their heritage.

conversion and the European act of criminalizing homosexuality sped up this process. It is because of this intentional destruction of culture that some tribes have lost their traditional views of gender. However, in recent years, many Native American LGBTQ+ activists have been working hard to educate others about the true history of third-gender people in their culture.

CHAPTER THREE

POLYNESIAN TRANSGENDER POPULATIONS

P olynesia is made up of over a thousand islands in the Pacific Ocean. Much like Native American tribes, Polynesia's many island nations all share cultural similarities while living under distinct governments.

Polynesian culture is largely based around fishing and sailing. Polynesia has a tropical climate. European sailors first described Polynesian peoples in Louis-Antoine de Bougainville's 1771 book, *Voyage Around the World*. Before that time, the various Polynesian cultures were isolated between approximately 700 CE and the eighteenth century.

Western merchants and sailors were the first people to encounter gender identities and presentation in Polynesian culture. Sources written by these westerners thus had a particular flavor of bias. Their writing was informed by religious and cultural limitations. After their first encounter with the West, Polynesian islanders were forced to adjust their view of gender roles. But that didn't keep modern scholars from piecing together the story of transgender people in that region.

FIXED OR SHIFTING PERSONAL IDENTITIES

Most of Western society considers a person's identity to be fixed: the impression is that a person's identity, self-made or imposed, stays relatively the same no matter what situation that person is in. This especially holds true for things like gender and sexuality. But in Polynesian culture, one's identity is less fixed.

Whereas European culture dictates that people's identities define how they act in social situations, Polynesian culture usually relied on personal

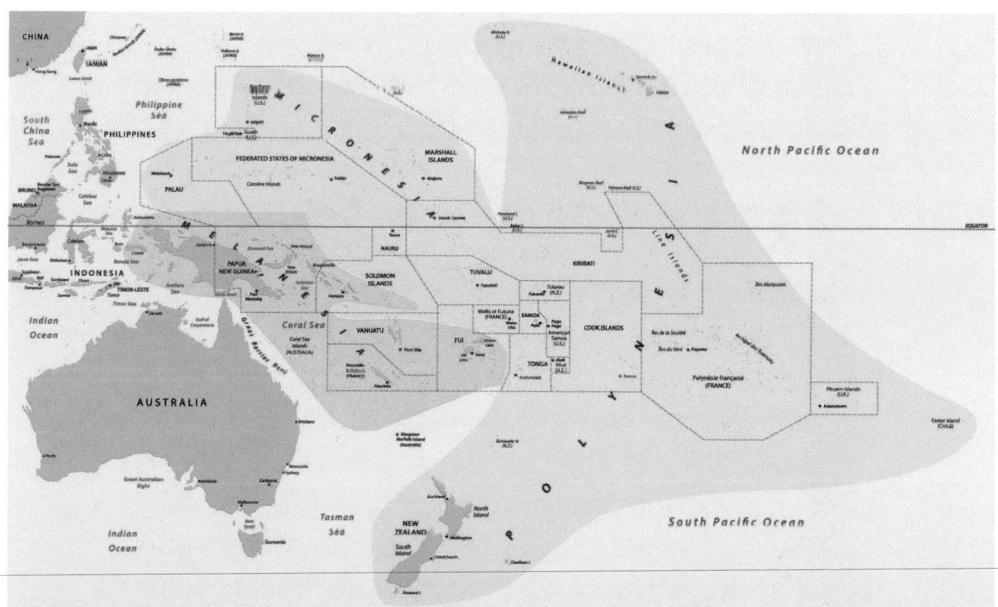

Polynesia refers to a group of over one thousand islands in the South Pacific Ocean. The countries in this region have many similarities, but they each have their own sovereign governments.

relationships within a social situation to regulate behavior. As such, Polynesians made room for an environment in which identity allowed people to interact based upon their sex and social class. Polynesians, especially men, can also behave in ways that are contrary to their gender roles. Constant transitioning between different roles for different reasons indicates fluidity. A less flexible fluidity may be due to a permanent role change.

The Polynesians' fluid view of identity also meant that what people did in private didn't necessarily affect how society viewed them. In most Western cultures, what one does in private affects how one is perceived socially, especially when it comes to things like gender and sexuality. Western society has even gone to great lengths to dictate private conduct as a means of defining decency. For Polynesians, private acts remained private. As long as people adhered to social norms in public, their private life generally would not affect them socially. Therefore, Polynesians placed more importance on how people acted within social situations than upon who people were as individuals.

Before Western exposure, some Polynesians viewed sexuality as a choice but recognized that gender was not. Still, it was thought that people who were born into the gender role of *mahu*, or third gender, might later choose to leave that role. People could also choose to have sex with either gender, as opposed to feeling compelled by attraction. Sexual choices were viewed as acceptable but controllable. People were not seen as being able to control or choose their gender. Because personal identity

KUMA HINA

In 2014, the documentary *Kuma Hina* premiered at the Hawaii International Film Festival. It follows the life of Hina Wong-Kalu, a transgender teacher in Hawaii. Wong-Kalu identifies as a mahu, which to her means someone who is "in the middle" between male and female.

The documentary explains the history of the mahu as Wong-Kalu counsels a student who is also what she calls "in-between." Wong-Kalu's student is anatomically female, demonstrating that not all mahu are male bodied.

The documentary was named Outstanding Documentary by the GLAAD Media Awards. It received many positive reviews and won awards at film festivals. The documentary has been included in an education campaign that raises awareness about gender nonbinary people. It was also featured on PBS.

mattered less in Polynesian culture than identity within the social group, identity was seen as something more likely to change.

MULTIPLE POLYNESIAN TRANSGENDER LABELS

In Hawaii and Tahiti, the term "mahu" has historically described individuals assigned male at

In 2016, Hina Wong-Kalu attends the Kamehameha Day Lei Draping. Two years earlier, Wong-Kalu was the subject of a documentary about being a mahu teacher in Hawaii.

birth who are nonbinary. Those originally assigned female were also called mahu because it basically signified a transgender identity. The mahu were expected to perform masculine and feminine roles. Even though they primarily dressed and acted in feminine ways, the mahu didn't entirely lose their masculinity. In fact, some mahu preferred to dress in more masculine ways. Mahu are considered to be a third gender.

Other island nations in Polynesia have used their own terms to describe nonbinary people. Some Tonga people have been known to use the term *fakaleiti*, meaning "like a lady," to identify effeminate men, but those who fit the description just refer to themselves as *leiti*, or "lady." Samoans used the term *fa'afafine* to describe third-gender people who embody male and female gender roles, while in Tuvalu the term *pinapinaaine* historically described those whose sex was male and gender was female.

An early sign that a child was transgender in each culture was the child's preference to play with the opposite sex. But to the Hawaiians, when determining if a child was gender nonconforming, it has always been important that a child acts in the role of the opposite sex while playing. Girls and boys were known to play different games based on the gender they were playing with, so if a boy preferred to play a game that typically only girls played, it would be taken as a sign of gender nonconformity.

Tafi Toleafoa (*right*), a fa'afafine, helps care for her niece at a Samoan family gathering in Alaska in this 2007 photo.

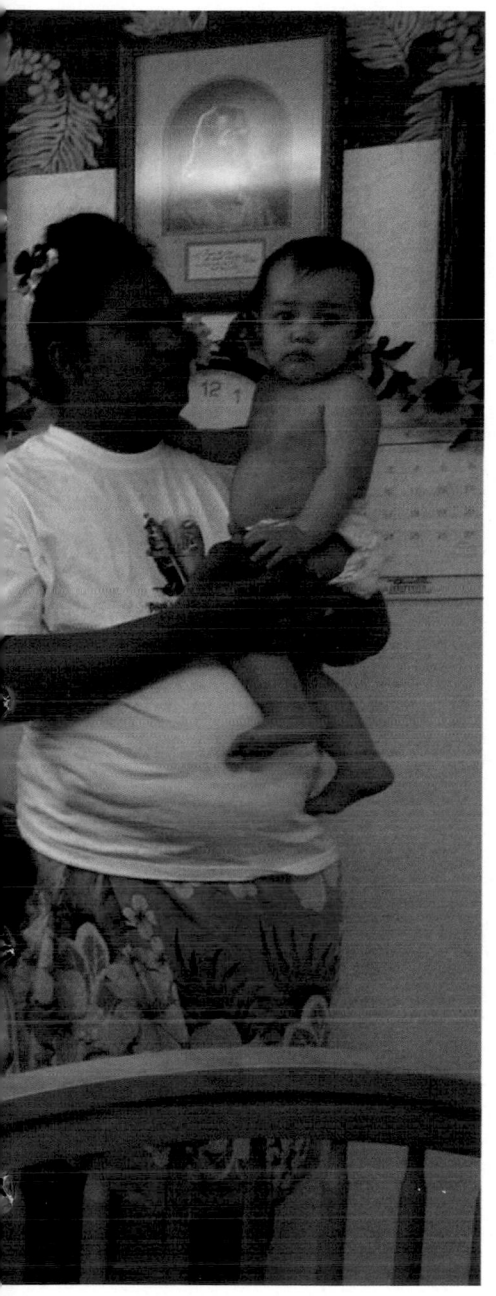

GENDER-NONCONFORMING FAMILIES AND SHIFTING ROLES

It was not uncommon for Samoan families that had no female children to encourage one of their boys to take on feminine roles in order to help the mother take care of the household. There are some cases of children being forced to take on gender-nonconforming roles, but mostly, children took on the roles willingly. Nonbinary people were valued because their unique ability to take on both gender roles meant that they could help with a greater number of household tasks. While acceptance was not universal, especially after colonization, most families encouragcd their nonbinary children to behave in a way that made them comfortable.

Miss Agu Tuinasau (*third from left*) is crowned Queen of Fiji's Adi Senikau pageant. It occurs in conjunction with the Hibiscus Festival.

MISS GALAXY PAGEANT

Beauty pageants are popular in many cultures. The Tonga Miss Galaxy pageant, in particular, is a beauty pageant for fakaleiti. Pageants like Miss Galaxy are not only fun places to play overly feminine roles, but they also provide participants with prestige.

Where most beauty pageants in Tonga emphasize the culture where each woman grew up, Miss Galaxy focuses more on gender performance. The pageants often include very suggestive dance routines that are meant to humorously portray how girls are not supposed to act. These morality lessons were considered socially appropriate only in mixed company if they came from the fakaleiti—fakaleiti can say things to a mixed

(continued on the next page)

(continued from the previous page)

group that would be seen as appropriate only in a homogenously gendered group.

In Samoa, the winner of the Miss Fa'afafine pageant also acts as a cultural ambassador. It is her job to help raise awareness of fa'afafine culture. Each year, the winner helps to highlight human rights issues in Samoa. They often focus on attempts to repeal antihomosexual laws that are still in place in many countries, including the United States.

Many gender-nonconforming people in Polynesia make money through performances like those given in the Miss Galaxy pageant. These acts call back to the kind of shows that were performed in Polynesia before Christian missionaries arrived.

Many third-gender people take on caretaker roles within their families. It's common for nonbinary people to care for their elderly parents and to help with any nieces and nephews they might have. As Polynesians traditionally value having large families, it's often necessary for parents to need help with their children from time to time. While heteronormative and cisnormative laws in some Polynesian nations make it difficult for nonbinary people to adopt children, many people are fighting to gain that right. Many nonbinary people do want to adopt children and do succeed at procreating.

While the mahu were not barred from participating in male roles in society, unmarried men were traditionally not taken seriously in certain roles. Being a husband and a father to many children was very important and elevated one's role in Polynesian society, but becoming the head of a household would mean leaving the mahu identity behind.

THE EFFECTS OF COLONIZATION

Many European sailors and colonists assumed that all mahu people were intersex. While some probably were, being intersex is not a defining characteristic of most nonbinary representations. An intersex person is one who is born with ambiguous genitalia, so it is unclear what their biological sex is. Usually, intersex people are assigned one gender at birth and socialized toward that gender's behavior. Intersex people were sometimes mistaken for eunuchs, men who had been castrated.

Polynesians didn't view having sex with a third-gender person as a sign of homosexuality because third-gender people were neither male nor female. They existed outside of the Western view of sex and gender. Regardless, many aspects of Polynesian culture were nearly lost entirely because of the efforts of Christian colonization. As Christianity spread on the islands, so, too, did intolerance of gender-nonconforming people, including the mahu.

Though contemporary Hawaiians are attempting to raise awareness of the history of the mahu, undoing centuries of intolerance will take time. Still, Hawaii is seen as one of the most socially liberal states. It is considered to be very friendly toward the LGBTQ+ community. Hawaii is currently one of the only states that allows transgender individuals to easily change the gender on their birth certificates.

CHAPTER FOUR

THE THIRD REICH

● ●

Berlin in the 1920s was the place to be if you were a sexual minority. Despite the fact that "homosexual acts" had been made illegal in the German Empire's penal code in 1872 under a law known as paragraph 175, the capital city of Berlin had many nightclubs and restaurants that catered to the gay community. In fact, queer people from all over the world came to Berlin for its accepting culture. There was some social and political resistance to paragraph 175; the first attempt to repeal the law happened in 1898. Many famous Germans such as scientist Albert Einstein, author Hermann Hesse, and painter Käthe Kollwitz publicly called for the law to be repealed. But the rise of Nazi Germany would halt LGBTQ+ progress.

THE INSTITUTE OF SEX RESEARCH

It was in this climate of relative tolerance that Dr. Magnus Hirschfeld, a sexologist, opened the Institute of Sex Research. The institute was a

This 1928 photo depicts German physician and sexologist Magnus Hirschfeld at the age of sixty.

library, a place of research, and a medical clinic. Psychiatry was a relatively new field of study at the time, so not much was known about human sexuality as a whole, let alone about sexual minorities. The Institute of Sex Research sought to change that.

Hirschfeld was one of the first advocates for the rights of transgender people. He believed that research could dispel myths about homosexuals and other sexual minorities and that through knowledge would come even more tolerance.

Hirschfeld was one of the first scientists to understand the difference between gender and sexuality. He understood that there was a difference between a man who is attracted to men and a transgender woman who is attracted to men. As a gay man, he believed that each person's presentation of gender and sexuality was unique and based on a variety of factors.

Hirschfeld, who invented the term "transvestite," lacked much of the vocabulary we now use to describe sex and gender. Despite having little preexisting language to work with, many of his early theories are consistent with current understandings. For example, while Hirschfeld's peers believed that there were only two sexualities and two genders, he believed the combinations of human gender and sex were much higher and had many more factors involved. He referred to these combinations as "sexual intermediaries" and thought they took into account everything from one's sexual preferences to cultural habits.

He was one of the first to advocate that not only should transgender people be allowed to present in the gender they stated they were but that this should be encouraged. He found that allowing his patients to present and be treated as members of the opposite gender helped to alleviate the negative feelings they had surrounding their gender identity.

Hirschfeld had a hard time convincing his medical peers of the value of his findings, but he did have some luck in convincing the Berlin police to stop targeting and harassing transgender women.

EARLY TRANS ADVOCACY

One of the first things that became clear to Hirschfeld and his staff as they began to advocate on behalf of trans people was how difficult it was for them to find work. The simplest solution that the doctors could come up with was to hire as many trans people to work for the institute as they could. Dora Richter, one of the transgender women who worked as a maid in the institute, would become the first recipient of vaginoplasty gender affirmation surgery under Hirschfeld's supervision in 1931.

A Danish transgender woman named Lili Elbe heard about Hirschfeld's work and sought him out. In 1930, she traveled to the Dresden's Women's Clinic and under Hirschfeld's supervision completed a different method of gender affirmation surgery in 1932. Elbe was also able to legally change her name and gender on her Danish identification.

Lili Elbe poses for a photo in 1931. Elbe was one of the first people to receive gender affirmation surgery. Ultimately, the process resulted in her body rejecting a uterine transplant.

The institute attracted doctors from all over the world. One doctor Hirschfeld befriended was Harry Benjamin, a German who immigrated to the

LILI ELBE

Einar Wegener lived as a man and as a painter but would come to call herself Lili Elbe. In 1904, Wegener married fellow art student Gerda Gottlieb, another painter. Wegener painted landscapes while Gottlieb focused on painting women's fashion.

One day, Gottlieb asked Wegener to pose as a female art model for her and to don women's clothing. This experience opened Wegener to her true identity. Around 1912, Wegener began to present as a woman and changed her name to Lili Elbe. She gave up painting as a part of Wegener's life.

It was shocking to some to learn that the iconic woman in Gottlieb's paintings was not what they knew to be a woman. Though Gottlieb was supportive of Elbe, the Danish government dissolved their marriage because same-sex marriage was illegal in Denmark. The couple remained friends, and Elbe was later proposed to by another friend. Elbe desperately wanted to give her husband a child, but as she was undergoing a uterus transplant, she got an infection and died of complications.

United States in 1913. Benjamin would continue Hirschfeld's transgender research in the United States. There, he would continue spreading his mentors' lesson that transgender people should be allowed to present as the gender of their choosing.

RISE OF THE THIRD REICH

In 1931, Hirschfeld left Germany on a book tour. Two years later, before he could return, Adolf Hitler was appointed chancellor of Germany. Hitler considered many people, including Jews and homosexuals, to be undesirable. He especially disliked Hirschfeld and referred to him as "the most dangerous Jew in Germany."

Knowing that returning to Germany would be dangerous, Hirschfeld never went back. He instead chose to live in Switzerland and hoped that the political climate would shift and allow him to continue his research. He willed the Institute of Sex Research to two of his contemporaries in the hopes that his research would continue.

On May 6, 1933, the Nazis occupied the institute. Hirschfeld's decades of research and the patient files the institute collected fell into Hitler's hands. On May 10, the contents of Hirschfeld's vast research library, along with the works of other authors deemed to be "enemies of Germany," were burned in a large bonfire. It was in a movie theater in Paris that Hirschfeld

This 1933 photo shows a group of Nazis in Berlin. One of them carries a bust of Dr. Hirschfeld on a stick as they go to burn down Hirschfeld's institute.

watched a newsreel of his life's work being destroyed.

By 1935, Hitler had expanded paragraph 175 to create more laws against homosexuals and those who participated in homosexual relations. Around fifty thousand men were arrested under paragraph 175, and somewhere between ten and fifteen thousand of those men were later sent to concentration camps.

While there is a rough estimate of how many people were sent to the camps solely for their sexuality, it is unclear how many LGBTQ+ people were sent to the camps for reasons other than their sexuality. It is also unknown how many transgender people were among those sent to concentration camps. Over 60 percent of those imprisoned in the camps for their sexuality did not survive.

The horrors of the Holocaust didn't end when the camps were liberated by the Allies. Even after the

PINK TRIANGLES

The Nazis were very organized and fond of categorizing their prisoners. One way they did this was to affix symbols to the prisoners' uniforms that explained why they were in the camps. Jews were given the yellow Star of David to wear, and homosexuals had to wear a pink triangle.

The camps could be especially dangerous for those wearing pink triangles. They were treated more harshly by the Nazi guards and were ostracized and sometimes antagonized by other prisoners who were homophobic.

In the late 1980s, the American AIDS activist group AIDS Coalition to Unleash Power (ACT UP) reclaimed the pink triangle. The group's purpose was to raise awareness about the government's inaction in the AIDS epidemic that killed thousands in the LGBTQ+ community. The pink triangle is still a sign of gay pride around the world.

war ended, homosexuality was still against the law in Germany. Many gay men and other members of the LGBTQ+ community who survived torture, starvation, and extreme conditions in the concentration camps found themselves sent to prison. Paragraph 175, though eased in 1969, was not repealed until 1994. Even so, the culture eventually swung back to its more tolerant days, and Berlin once again became known as a queer-friendly city. In 1980, a law was passed allowing trans people to change their legal sex only after sex reassignment surgery and compulsory sterilization. Both requirements

Homosexual prisoners wear the pink triangle in the Sachsenhausen concentration camp in Germany in this 1938 photo. Sachsenhausen was a camp where political enemies of Germany were kept, along with others.

were ruled unconstitutional in 2011. In 2013, it was ruled that intersex individuals could leave the gender on their birth certificates blank. This solved the problem of doctors having to decide the gender of an intersex child without the child's input. These legal steps are considered promising movements toward equality for trans individuals.

CHAPTER FIVE

TRANSGENDER AMERICA

J ust like their Protestant and Catholic predecessors, men and women in early American history had strictly defined roles that included everything from how one dressed to what jobs they could hold. These roles also came with the assumption that men were superior to women. Therefore, any threat to gender roles was also a threat to male superiority.

By 1850, well after American independence was established, many cities in the United States had outlawed cross-dressing, or the wearing of the opposite gender's clothes, in order to uphold traditional views. To change these roles to make space for people who didn't hold cisgender or heteronormative identities thus meant changing the very nature of society. There would be many individuals and collectives that were eager to take up this task so that they could live their identities.

CORRECTING NATURE

When Christine Jorgensen returned home to America in February 1953, no one could have predicted the instant spotlight her gender affirmation surgery would thrust her into. "EX-GI Becomes Blond Bombshell," read the *Daily News* headline in December 1952. But there was more. Jorgensen became an overnight celebrity who turned this attention into a successful show-business career. In her personal life, to explain her need for the surgery, Jorgensen wrote to her parents, "Nature made a mistake that I have corrected."

Even though gender affirmation surgeries had been taking place in Europe since Lili Elbe's surgery, which occurred between 1930 and 1932, many Americans had never heard of the procedure. Jorgensen was met with a mix of curiosity and disdain. To many, she was a medical oddity and was viewed as a kind of amusing sideshow. To others, she was an abomination, a sign that American society was falling apart.

American society had undergone a number of changes since World War II, and for many, Jorgensen seemed like a frightening culmination of them all. During World War II, women had left behind their previous gender roles and entered the workforce in unheard of numbers in order to replace the male workers who were overseas fighting in the military. After the war ended, many women had a hard time with the expectation that they would

DAILY NEWS

NEW YORK'S PICTURE NEWSPAPER○

FINAL

4¢

Vol. 34. No. 136   Copr. 1952 News Syndicate Co. Inc.   New York 17, N.Y., Monday, December 1, 1952*   4¢ IN CITY LIMITS 5¢ OUTSIDE CITY LIMITS

EX-GI BECOMES BLONDE BEAUTY

Operations Transform Bronx Youth

————Story on Page 3

[NEWS foto Copyright 1952 by NEWS Syndicate Co. Inc.]

A World of a Difference

George W. Jorgensen Jr., son of a Bronx carpenter, served in the Army [▲] for two years and was given honorable discharge in 1946. Now George is no more. After six operations, Jorgensen's sex has been changed and today she is a striking woman [◄—], working as a photographer in Denmark. Parents were informed of the big change in a letter Christine (that's her new name) sent to them recently.   *—Story on page 3*

This *Daily News* headline introduced Christine Jorgensen to the spotlight when she returned to the United States after her gender affirmation surgery.

return to the domestic lives they had lived before the war. They had gotten a taste of independence, and they liked it.

To those who were trying to return America to its strict prewar gender roles, Jorgensen was a unique threat. Few things were perceived as more masculine than the American GI. But if one could so easily be "turned into" an attractive and charming young woman, what did that say about manhood? While Jorgensen was never a political activist, her existence helped change how Americans perceived gender. Jorgensen's success and the relative acceptance of her was an inspiration to many trans people. When it was time for the children of the fifties to start shaping American culture, many trans people would demand a place in that culture as well.

POLICING THE TENDERLOIN

The 1960s were a turbulent time in American history. The country was in the midst of a highly controversial war in Vietnam, and the civil rights and women's rights movements were helping to challenge conventional views of society. The fight for equality was on everyone's minds, including for transgender people. Life for transgender people in America had never been easy, but the 1960s brought something new to the table: the possibility of winning the fight for one's rights.

Trans people weren't a common sight in most geographic areas in America, but larger cities, like

HOSE AND HEELS CLUB

Before the invention of the internet, it was very hard for gender-nonconforming and trans people to find each other. Coming out as one's true self could mean risking a violent encounter or even prison time. But pioneers of gender rights like Virginia Prince, who eventually decided to live her identity by presenting as a woman on a permanent basis, sought to change that.

In 1960, Prince published a magazine called *Transvestia*. In 1961, she invited a group of subscribers (it is unclear if they identified as transgender women or as men) who were gender nonconformists to bring a pair of stockings and high heels to a meeting at a hotel in Los Angeles. As a way of destigmatizing the act, she asked them all to put the hose and heels on together. It was the first time many of them had dressed contrarily to their sex in public, an act that was still illegal. One year later, the subscription list from her magazine would serve as the membership base for the Hose and Heels Club in Los Angeles.

Prince would eventually turn the Hose and Heels Club into the Foundation for Personality Expression, the first national group to address transgender issues.

New York and San Francisco, had growing LGBTQ+ communities. But the fact that these communities had a presence didn't mean they existed free of harassment. Police especially targeted transgender women. Those women often faced arrest and prostitution charges simply for being outside in gender-nonconforming clothing. As one of the most discriminated against segments of society, trans women's complaints about police brutality would largely go ignored.

By 1966, transgender women, unwelcome in most bars, took to hanging out in twenty-four-

VANGUARD

Community organizing was an important part of the civil rights movements in the 1960s. In San Francisco, a group of LGBTQ+ street kids decided they were going to be the change their community needed. In 1966, they formed a group called Vanguard, a self-styled "organization of, by and for the kids on the street."

The Vanguard was the first organization of its kind. These youths saw the streets as their home, and they wanted to clean it up and protect members of their community. In a time of great racial tension in the country, they urged people not to let race separate them. They especially focused on protecting trans women because they were so oppressed by the police. Members of Vanguard would play a large role in the Compton's Cafeteria riot.

hour restaurants like Compton's Cafeteria in San Francisco's Tenderloin District. The restaurant staff frequently got irritated that trans women would spend a long time in the restaurant while ordering very little. They often decided to combat this frugal patronage by calling the police to come harass the women.

Things between these trans women and the police came to a head early in August of that year at Compton's Cafeteria. A police officer with a reputation for being rough on trans women attempted to arrest one of the restaurant's patrons. Her response was to throw her coffee in his face. Many of the trans and queer clientele of this packed restaurant joined in throwing everything from purses to food trays at police. By the time the commotion had ended, people had smashed a picture widow, burned down a newsstand, and vandalized a police car.

Even though no newspapers covered the riot at Compton's Cafeteria, it influenced the creation of the Central City Anti-Poverty Program. This organization appointed Officer Elliot Blackstone as a liaison to the LGBTQ+ community.

When transgender community organizer Louise Ergestrasse demanded that Officer Blackstone do something to help them, Blackstone listened. He worked hard to understand the LGBTQ+ people he was tasked with serving. He did his best to convince police not to arrest trans women simply for using bathrooms that matched their gender. With Blackstone's help, things got marginally better for the

This photo shows Elliott Blackstone in 1971. He was the police liaison to San Francisco's LGBTQ+ community and one of the first officers to fight for gender and sexual minorities.

LGBTQ+ community in San Francisco.

DO SOMETHING

The patrons of gay bars were no strangers to police harassment. It wasn't very long before 1969 that it was illegal for bars to serve gay people. There was also the fact that at the time, New York did still have cross-dressing laws. Anyone found in a bar wearing clothing of the opposite sex would be arrested. Cross-dressing women or transgender men, for example, had to be wearing three feminine articles of clothing to avoid arrest. It was a common tactic during police raids of the time to take anyone wearing women's clothing to the bathroom and force them to show their genitals.

In spite of earlier signs of discontent, a 1969 riot in New York City stemming from one of these bar raids would spark a countrywide movement for gay rights. On June 28 of that year, the police raided one of the most popular gay bars in the city, the Stonewall Inn. On this occasion, there were nearly two hundred queer people in the bar and only eight police officers.

Usually, such a small number of officers would be adequate to manage arresting patrons and evacuating the bar, but something about this night was different—the queer patrons of the Stonewall Inn had had enough.

The police allowed about 150 people to leave the bar, but the crowd didn't disperse. Instead, they waited outside. When the police wagons arrived, there weren't enough

Storme DeLarverie sits between old photos of herself. She was a cross-dresser and lesbian who is often credited with throwing the first punch during the Stonewall riots.

of them to hold everyone that had been arrested. Some people had to wait longer to be taken to jail.

As the police attempted to fill the first wagon, someone, possibly Storme DeLarverie, managed to escape the wagon four or five times. Each time, she was hit and dragged back. Finally, bleeding from a head wound, she turned to the crowd and yelled, "Why don't you guys do something?" After the police hurled her into the van again, the crowd outside erupted, throwing coins, bottles, whatever was around.

Fighting began in the bar, too. Some think it started after African American drag queen Marsha P. Johnson yelled, "I got my civil rights!" and hurled a shot glass at a mirror. Regardless of what started it, everything inside would be destroyed. Many refer to it as "the shot glass heard 'round the world."

For a long time, the Stonewall riots were portrayed or described as crowds of gay men responding to police brutality, but it's now known that lesbians and transgender people were influential in the events as well. As for other parts of its legacy, it's important to remember that the Stonewall riots began the birth of not just the gay rights movement but the movement for transgender rights as well.

CHAPTER SIX

HIJRAS

∙∙

In India, where the majority of Hindus originate, the concept of a third gender, or *hijra*, has been widely accepted from ancient times until the British government's occupation of the Indian subcontinent in 1858. The occupying British colonial authority passed antisodomy laws in an attempt to legislate hijras into extinction. These attempts failed to eradicate the hijra population, and hijras retained their roles in society even under the threat of legal action.

WHAT A HIJRA IS

This third gender, called hijra, is neither man nor woman, although the term applies only to those who were initially assigned male at birth. Homosexual men are considered separate from hijras. Hijras have held a special place in society on the Indian subcontinent for four thousand years.

A hijra generally identifies as being neither a man nor a woman but outwardly presents as

Telangana Hijra Intersex Transgender Samiti activists protest to gain recognition. Discrimination against hijras persists despite the Supreme Court of India's 2014 ruling in favor of hijra recognition.

female. Hijras use female pronouns and wear feminine clothing to signify identifying with the feminine.

Hijras are generally assumed to be sexually impotent, but not all sexually impotent men are hijras. Few hijras are truly impotent. Many believe that all hijras have their genitalia removed as part of a ritual known as *nirwaan*, but less than 8 percent of hijras in India actually undergo this ritual. Those who do treat the ritual as a sign of devotion to the Hindu goddess Bahuchara Mata, a hijra figure that many hijras worship.

Akin to hijras, though there are far fewer in the population, are the *sadhin*. Their low numbers may be because children born with female genitalia must decide they want to become sadhin at an early age. It is the only chance they have to truly be considered sadhin. Usually, before the onset of menstruation, they must decide they are neither female nor male. The sadhin are believed to transcend gender, and they are also thought to be asexual.

A girl must be a virgin if she wants to become a sadhin. In transcending gender, they are renouncing marriage and sexuality. While there is no ritual to mark the occasion, once the sadhin begin to wear masculine clothing and cut their hair short they are recognized as having transcended. They still participate in some female jobs, but during gender-segregated ceremonies the sadhin are allowed to sit with the men. They are also allowed to make offerings to ancestors that are reserved for sons. They are viewed with less fear than hijras. They are also not considered to have any special spiritual power.

HIJRAS AFTER COLONIALISM

Hijras occupied and continue to hold a complex role in Indian society. While Indian society at large often views hijras with apprehension and fear, they have an important role in society and are usually respected.

It is considered to confer a blessing of fertility when a hijra performs at a wedding or a ceremony for the birth of a child. Their performances often

Hindu deity Bahuchara Mata sits atop a rooster. She holds a sword, scriptures, a trident, and blessings. Many hijra feel a special connection with this deity.

include funny songs and dances poking fun at relationship tensions. These performances are sometimes sexually graphic. Requested or not, it's considered good luck to pay hijras at the end of the ceremony. If hijras are not paid, they can remove a blessing just as easily as they offered it.

Some believe that hijras have the power to curse a family line with infertility by lifting their skirts. This belief leads some to be wary of hijras, but they are generally seen as a part of the community.

Hijras have also been faced with verbal and occasionally violent harassment due to people's

BAHUCHARA MATA

Bahuchara Mata is a mother goddess who rides upon a rooster. Many stories tie the goddess to acts of castration either as punishment or as a sign of devotion.

Some hijras feel called by the goddess to participate in the nirwaan ritual. They fear that not heeding the call would result in being cursed with impotence for the next seven reincarnations. Some see the ritual as a way to renounce sexual desire and become a vessel for Bahuchara Mata's power.

Sometimes, after a hijra has healed from the nirwaan, they are dressed in wedding clothes and paraded around the town as a sign that the transition from incomplete to complete has occurred. While there are no records as to how common this ritual was prior to the British occupation, it is now very uncommon for hijras to have such a procedure done.

fear of them. This fear stems from the power many believe hijras hold. As with many Native American tribes, Hindus believe that as devotees of Bahuchara Mata, hijras have spiritual power.

Hijras' feminine clothing never bothered the general public before the British occupation began in 1858. For a time during British rule, an occupying British king had demanded they wear a man's turban along with their feminine clothing, but otherwise, their wardrobe was not policed.

However, British colonists brought even more intolerance into Indian culture. In 1897, British colonists passed a law criminalizing eunuchs. They perceived hijras as eunuchs and condemned hijras under this law accordingly. This ostracized hirjas from their communities and families. Laws against homosexual acts were also passed, serving to further punish hijras who chose to have sexual relationships with men.

DOMESTIC LIFE

While some hijras do have husbands, most live in communal houses with other hijras. These houses can have anywhere from five to twenty-five hijras of all ages living together. Hijras in communal houses share household responsibilities like cooking and cleaning. They share their income and contribute toward managing the house.

These houses have become a sort of family for hijras. Each house acts as an "ancestor" for hijras.

A *naik*, or chief, runs the house. Newcomers to the house are referred to as *chelas* (disciples), and each is given a teacher called a guru. The guru is obligated to take care of their chela, just as a mother takes care of a daughter. Gurus record the names of each chela in the house record book. This community creates an extended family for hijras. Although it is common for hijras to migrate from house to house, these family lines remain intact.

The houses often control what jobs hijras can do in the community. It can have a significantly negative economic impact on a hijra if she isn't allowed to work. Some of these houses take advantage of young hijras and force them into dangerous work, like prostitution.

Children play lezims, small instruments with cymbals, at a school in Panvel, India. A child of about this age could opt to be considered a sadhin.

HIJRAS IN MODERN TIMES

Upon gaining its independence from Britain in 1947, India did not completely revert back to its original attitude toward hijras.

A 2014 Indian Supreme Court ruling stated that hijras and other transgender people could list a third gender on official documents, but it offered no protection from the rampant discrimination that arose from British colonial rule, and the court's ruling failed to address rights concerning marriage, adoption, property inheritance, and other legal protections other Indians are guaranteed. The Supreme Court's mandated recognition of hijra identities thus has strict limitations on how much it could offer to the advancement of Indian hijra populations.

Pakistan's and India's historical treatment of hijras after British occupation was similar in areas like discrimination and familial rejection. However, the more current treatment of hijras in Pakistan— as far as the government is concerned—differs greatly. According to the Foreign Policy Group, hijras have of late acquired a good number of rights that parallel their cisgender counterparts due to the 2009 ruling in *Khaki v. Rawalpindi*: "the Supreme Court for the first time in the history of Pakistan, granted the transgender community their own gender category under Pakistan's National Database and Registration Authority (NADRA)..." Where the Indian government stopped at recognizing hijra identities (and compelled them to label themselves as a third sex instead of one of the binary sexes when reregistering their identity), the Pakistani government offered a more comprehensive integration plan that sought to facilitate "acceptance, implementation and rehabilitation." The government ordered the creation of mechanisms that would protect and enable hijras' inheritance rights, employment, and election registration, with measures like educating them so that they could successfully satisfy the requirements of various jobs, giving them preference for jobs that their established skill set fit into, and tracking down their families so that they wouldn't be passed over in cases of inheritance. Police were ordered to stop harassing them, and systems were created to prosecute members of law enforcement who participated in unacceptable conduct against them. All of this has occurred in spite of Pakistan's modern-era track record of treating sexual minorities with violent contempt on a political and social level.

While these changes sound great, getting society to follow along with them is generally never easy. But the government's holistic support speaks volumes to the new potential for hijras in Pakistan. The act of designating a timeline for when various institutions were expected to comply with the court's orders means that the government had a sense of urgency in solving the problems of the hijra community and a sense of sincerity concerning acknowledging hijras' rights. The Pakistani government's actions serve as a great model for reparations that takes into account the special needs of an oppressed group while offering hope that the oppressed group will one day fully recover from the wrongs it once received.

CHAPTER SEVEN

THE FUTURE IS NONBINARY

To many, the current change in gender roles and the societal understanding of gender may seem new. However, how we think about gender is constantly evolving. When American women entered the workforce in large numbers, in the 1940s, it was considered revolutionary. Not anymore! It's currently expected that women will work outside the home. Allowing gender roles and the understanding of gender to change gives everyone a chance to pursue the self that makes them feel most whole and complete.

HOLLYWOOD HITS AND MISSES

In June 2014, the cover of *Time* magazine featured a photo of Laverne Cox. She was the first transgender woman to appear on the cover of the magazine. Cox became famous for playing Sophia, a transgender woman in jail for credit card fraud, on the show *Orange Is the New Black*.

Laverne Cox appears at the Netflix FYSee Kick Off Event in 2017. Cox represents the transgender community in the media in a way that humanizes an otherwise marginalized population.

For many, Sophia brought awareness of transgender issues into American homes for the first time. Viewers were able to see Sophia as a person rather than as an abstract concept. This kind of empathy helps people accept those who are different. As our understanding of and language used for gender evolves, so does the way our society views gender.

Since Laverne Cox successfully brought Sophia to the small screen, other movies and television shows have also added transgender and nonbinary characters to their productions. For the first time in American history, underrepresented genders are being portrayed positively and more accurately than ever before in the media. Accurate portrayals of all genders bring people one step closer to dismissing their assumptions and stereotypes and seeing people for who they really are. Activists hope that this kind of media representation will help people to understand the queer community more and help protect their rights.

While there are still relatively few movies and TV shows that have transgender or gender-nonconforming characters, the ones that are coming out are well liked both by audiences and critics. *Dallas Buyers Club* (2013) and *The Danish Girl* (2015) both featured transgender women as main characters and were nominated for Oscars.

Jared Leto and Eddie Redmayne, the two cisgender male actors who played the transgender women in those movies, respectively, were also nominated for Oscars. However, some people criticized the movies for giving the roles of trans women to cisgender men. There are still very few roles for gender-nonconforming people in the movie industry, so when transgender roles go to cisgender actors, it makes the industry less inclusive of others. It's important to allow marginalized groups the ability to tell their own stories. It offers a more authentic view of their lives. When the media accurately portrays the many different types of people in the world, it helps everyone feel accepted

AMANDLA STENBERG

Amandla is the Zulu word for "power," something that Amandla Stenberg exudes. At age four, Stenberg began modeling and soon began acting as well. Stenberg's breakout role was as the character Rue in *The Hunger Games* (2012).

In a post on Stenberg's personal blog in 2016, the actress, who had already come out as bisexual, also revealed that they were nonbinary and preferred they/them over she/her pronouns. After Stenberg announced their gender, fans changed all of the pronouns on Stenberg's Wikipedia page as a sign of respect. Stenberg asked them to change the pronouns back to female ones. While Stenberg prefers they/them pronouns, it was easier to get work using she/her pronouns. This is a sign of the pervasive

(continued on the next page)

Actress Amandla Stenberg attends a screening of *Everything, Everything* at the TCL Chinese Theatre in Hollywood, California.

(continued from the previous page)

intolerance that gender-nonconforming people face in the workforce. Finding jobs that are accepting of gender nonconformity is difficult, even for people who are as famous and talented as Stenberg.

When Stenberg isn't busy acting, they use the platform fame has given them to be an activist. Stenberg is also a musician who released an album of themselves singing and playing the violin.

and creates more space for creative and realistic stories to be told.

Young adult and graphic novels have also presented more gender-nonconforming characters. DC Comics introduced the first transgender comic character. In issue 45 of *Batgirl*, the title character, Barbara Gordon, meets her new roommate, a transgender woman named Alysia Yeoh. Barbara later goes on to be a bridesmaid at Alysia's wedding. The comic book *Saga* by Brian K. Vaughn includes transgender characters in its epic space odyssey that deals heavily with issues of prejudice and the need for acceptance. The comic has been praised for its large, diverse cast of characters. The book *If I Was Your Girl* by Meredith Russo tells the story of a transgender

THE SIMS

Even video games are catching on to the fact that gender is a spectrum. *The Sims* is one of the most popular video games ever made. It is a life simulator that allows players to create characters and have them go about their daily lives. Players can follow characters from their birth all the way until they pass away of old age. *The Sims 4* was designed to show gender outside of the binary model. Whereas earlier editions only allowed players to choose between male and female characters and make their looks match traditionally male or female clothing and hairstyles, those restrictions no longer apply. Players can gender-bend their characters' looks. These kinds of changes allow everyone to create more authentic versions of themselves within the game. Many fans loved that these changes allowed them even more options and ways to play the game.

girl named Amanda starting over at a new school. It won the ALA Stonewall Book Award in 2016. It's been hailed by many as a book that all teens should read because of its theme of being true to yourself.

CHANGING LAWS

As America becomes more aware of transgender and nonbinary people, efforts to ensure that everyone has a place in society continue to make progress, albeit slowly. Bathroom bills have passed in many states. Some states want to protect the rights of transgender people to use the bathroom that matches their gender identity. Others, however, have gone in the opposite direction and have tried to legislate that people must use the bathroom that matches the sex listed on their birth certificate. North Carolina passed the most notable of such bills in March 2016. The Public Facilities Privacy & Security Act, also called HB2, dictates that people must use the bathroom that matches their sex. That law also prevents cities from raising their minimum wage to higher than the state's, and it repealed the state's LGBTQ+ antidiscrimination laws.

While rural, conservative areas of the state tended to support the bill, urban areas opposed it. However, the wider public response to North Carolina's bill was immediate and largely negative. Businesses all over the United States that opposed the measure began to take away jobs and contracts from the state. PayPal, which had been planning to open offices in the state, decided to go elsewhere to ensure that none of its employees would face discrimination because of their gender. The amount of revenue brought to the state through tourism also dropped. Many visitors either no longer felt welcome or were inclined to protest the state's discriminatination against a minority. Artists, sports teams, and theater companies also refused to hold events in North Carolina. On top of that, the legal drama just began after HB2 was passed. Several discrimination lawsuits were filed.

In March 2017, after a year of lawsuits both in support of and against HB2, it was repealed. However, the law that repealed HB2 still prevents cities in North Carolina from passing nondiscrimination ordinances to protect LGBTQ+ people until December 2020. Some feel the new law is unclear and likely to be legally challenged again.

At roughly the same time, the Supreme Court agreed to hear the case of Gavin Grimm in what many hoped would be a landmark ruling for the transgender community. Grimm is a transgender boy who was banned from using the boy's bathroom at his high school. Grimm's lawyers argued that the school ban violated Title IX, which prevents students from being discriminated against based on their sex. However, after President Trump rescinded an order by President Obama for public schools to allow students to use the bathroom that matches their gender identity, the Supreme Court decided not to hear Grimm's case. The court also overturned a previous court order that had allowed Grimm to use the boy's room at his school. Despite this setback, transgender advocates were encouraged by the progress

This 2016 photo shows transgender teen Gavin Grimm with his mom, Deirdre Grimm, in Gloucester, Virginia.

of other similar cases in federal court and hopeful that transgender students' right to use the bathroom that matched their identity would be protected in the future.

THE FUTURE OF GENDER

Gender has always meant different things to different cultures. While there are many similarities across cultures and time periods, there are notable differences as well. However, gender is more complicated than binary thinking makes it out to be. While the terms people use may have changed over time, the fact remains that gender has always encompassed more than the two mutually exclusive male and female identities.

Back when police were arresting people at the Stonewall Inn, it was common practice to check that a person's clothes matched his or her sex. After this degrading search, anyone deemed to be cross-dressing would be arrested. Now, discrimination based solely on one's clothing is far less common.

As more people feel safe to express their true gender, it will become more apparent to those who aren't already aware that many of the expectations concerning gender are arbitrary. Things like jobs and hobbies have already become less associated with gender than they were in the past in most Western cultures.

But some institutions still don't contribute to the advancement of gender equality. The *Diagnostic and Statistical Manual of Mental Disorders II (DSM-II)* was the first edition of that volume to exclude homosexuality from being designated a mental disorder. Yet, there are two forms of transgender identities, gender dysphoria and transvestitism, that are still included. In other words, being transgender is still categorized as a mental illness, with implications that the transgender identity should be cured. While conversion therapy is no longer an acceptable medical standard, the original association of the *DSM* with conversion therapy is a perfect example of long-lasting stigmas.

There is still a long way to go for gender-nonconfirming people to feel included and have

A protestor holds a sign at a Chicago rally for transgender rights in 2017. Like many other countries, the United States has a long way to go in improving its record of human rights for transgender people.

their civil rights protected in all areas of life, including medicine, housing, employment, and legislation. Social spaces that can often be more inclusive in various societies include families, schools, and houses of worship.

To be successful in life, transgender people need the people around them to support them, just as anyone functions well when they can rely on society at large. That means that they are not the ones who need to change. Through self-education and learning with others about the many genders that exist, the world can become a more welcoming and livable place for all.

TIMELINE

1850s Many American states begin to pass laws that criminalize cross-dressing.

1890s Osh-Tisch and other two-spirit Native Americans are jailed and forced to perform hard labor as punishment for their gender nonconformity.

1897 The British rulers of the Indias subcontinent pass laws criminalizing eunuchs.

1919 Magnus Hirschfeld opens the Institute of Sex Research in Germany.

1931 Lili Elbe has gender affirmation surgery in Germany.

1933 Dr. Hirschfeld is unable to return to Germany. Nazis occupy the Institute of Sex Research.

1952 Christine Jorgensen becomes famous for receiving gender affirmation surgery.

1960 Vanguard, a community organization, is formed in San Francisco to protect street youth and LGBTQ+ individuals.

Virginia Prince starts the Hose and Heels Club, the first support group for cross-dressing men in the United States.

1966 The Compton Cafeteria riot occurs in San Francisco. This was one of the first times that transgender and gender-nonconforming people stood up for their rights.

1969 The Stonewall riots begin the LGBTQ+ rights movement in New York City.

1980 Germany passes a law allowing transgender individuals to change the gender on their birth certificates.

1999 The first Transgender Day of Remembrance occurs, honoring Rita Hester.

2014 The documentary *Kuma Hina* debuts to great critical success.

India officially recognizes third-gender individuals on official documents.

Laverne Cox is the first transgender woman to be on the cover of *Time* magazine.

2016 North Carolina passes the controversial Public Facilities Privacy & Security Act, also known as HB2.

2017 Dandara Dos Santos is beaten and murdered, sparking national outrage in Brazil.

The Supreme Court of the United States sends Gavin Grimm's case back to the Fourth Circuit Court of Appeals.

North Carolina's HB2 bill is partially repealed.

GLOSSARY

assimilate To ignore one's own culture in order to fit into the dominant culture.

cisgender Someone whose sex and gender identity are the same.

conversion therapy A condemned medical practice that tries to convince a queer person that they are cisgender and/or heterosexual.

corporal punishment Physical punishment, like hitting, as a penalty for some offense.

cross-dressing The act of dressing like the opposite gender, usually in a private, less showy manner than drag.

drag queen A man who dresses in women's clothes, usually in an exaggerated feminine style, as a performance.

fluidity The amount of malleability of one's sexuality, gender, or some other aspect of one's personality.

gender A psychological identity that derives from holding traits that are masculine, feminine, and/or of a gender that doesn't fit the binary.

gender affirmation surgery A surgery that is meant to change one's sexual organs and breasts in order to match that person's gender identity.

gender nonconforming Describing someone who does not act according to or who doesn't fit into society's prescribed gender roles.

heterosexual Being sexually attracted to the opposite sex.

hijra A person in India who was assigned male at

birth but who identifies as neither male nor female.

homosexual Being sexually attracted to the same sex; historically, being gay (even before the word "homosexual" was common) was equated to nonconforming performances of gender.

intersex Describes a person who has genitals and/or sex organs of either both sexes or that is ambiguous (cannot be clearly defined as male or female).

mahu A Hawaiian person whose gender identity does not fit into the gender binary.

nirwaan The Hindu ritual of removing the penis, scrotum, and testicles.

nonbinary Describes a person who is neither male nor female or who perhaps identifies with both genders.

sadhin An Indian term for a transgender man who was allowed to transition at a young age.

sex The biological traits associated with male identity or female identity, like genitalia and the presentation of the twenty-third pair of chromosomes (XX, XY, and less common configurations).

sexologist A scientist who studies sexuality and sexual expression.

street harassment One-sided, public flirting with a passerby who isn't interested. Particularly extreme street harassment crosses the line from verbal action to attempted touching, especially without the affirmative consent of the passerby.

third gender A term that refers to different genders that aren't exclusively male or female.

transgender A term for people who feel their sex and gender are not the same.

travesti A word that sometimes has derogatory connotations, it is a Latin American term for male-bodied nonbinary people.

two-spirit The term for Native American transgender and nonbinary people.

FOR MORE INFORMATION

The Ali Forney Center (AFC)
321 West 125th Street
New York, NY 10027
(212) 206-0574
Website: http://www.aliforneycenter.org
Facebook: @AliForney
Twitter: @AliForneyCenter
The AFC is the largest organization in the United
States dedicated to providing resources,
including housing, job preparedness, and
health care services, for LGBTQ+ youth who
are homeless.

The Center
208 West 13th Street
New York, NY 10011
(212) 620-7310
Website: https://gaycenter.org
Facebook: @lgbtcenternyc
Twitter: @LGBTCenterNYC
The Center offers community space and resources
to the LGBTQ+ community in New York City.

GLSEN
110 William Street, 30th Floor
New York, NY 10038
(212) 727-0135
Website: https://www.glsen.org
Facebook and Twitter: @GLSEN
Instagram: @glsenofficial

This national student organization is devoted to making schools safer for LGBTQ+ students.

Rainbow Health Ontario
Sherbourne Health Centre
333 Sherbourne Street
Toronto, ON M5A 2S5
Canada
(416) 324-4100
Website: http://www.rainbowhealthontario.ca
Facebook: @RainbowHealthOntario
Twitter: @RainbowHealthOn
This organization works to make health services more accessible to the Ontario community.

Sylvia Rivera Law Project (SRLP)
147 West 24th Street, 5th Floor
New York, NY 10011
(212) 337-8550
Website: https://srlp.org
Facebook: @SylviaRiveraLawProject
Twitter: @srlp
Instagram: @sylviariveralawproject
This group provides legal assistance to transgender youth so that they can live without discrimination.

Trans Youth Equality Foundation
PO Box 7441
Portland, ME 04112
(207) 478-4087
Website: http://www.transyouthequality.org
Facebook: @transyouthequality

Twitter: @TYEFofficial
Tumblr: @transyouthequality
This foundation advocates for the rights and needs
of transgender youth through education and
awareness campaigns.

Triangle Program
115 Simpson Avenue
Toronto, ON M4K 1A1
Canada
(416) 393-8443
Website: http://triangleprogram.ca
Facebook: @The-Triangle-Program
This is Canada's only high school just for LGBTQ+
students.

FOR FURTHER READING

Andrews, Arin. *Some Assembly Required: The Not-So-Secret Life of a Transgender Teen*. New York, NY: Simon and Schuster, 2015.

Bausum, Ann. *Stonewall: Breaking Out in the Fight for Gay Rights*. New York, NY: Penguin Group, 2016.

Klein, Rebecca T. *Transgender Rights and Protections* (Transgender Life). New York, NY: Rosen Publishing: 2017.

Kuklin, Susan. *Beyond Magenta: Transgender Teens Speak Out*. Somerville, MA: Candlewick Press, 2014.

Mardell, Ashley. *The ABC's of LGBT+*. Coral Gables, FL: Mango Media, 2016.

Meyer, Susan. *Health Issues When You're Transgender* (Transgender Life). New York, NY: Rosen Publishing, 2017.

Nut, Amy Ellis. *Becoming Nicole: The Transformation of an American Family*. New York, NY: Random House, 2015.

Setterington, Ken. *Branded by the Pink Triangle*. Toronto, CA: Second Story Press, 2013.

Teich, Nicholas M., and Jamison Green. *Transgender 101: A Simple Guide to a Complex Issue*. New York, NY: Columbia University Press, 2012.

Tosh, Jemma. *Psychology and Gender Dysphoria: Feminist and Transgender Perspectives*. London, UK: Routledge, 2016.

Wilcox, Christine. *Teens and LGBT Issues*. San Diego, CA: Referencepoint Press, 2015.

BIBLIOGRAPHY

Allen, Mercedes. "Transgender History: Trans Expression in Ancient Times." The Bilerico Project, February 12, 2008. http://bilerico .lgbtqnation.com/2008/02/transgender _history_trans_expression_in.php.

AntiJen Pages. "Luiza Bambine Moreira—'Roberta Close.'" September 2003. http://www.antijen .org/Articles/RC1.html.

Associated Press. "India Recognises Transgender People as Third Gender." *Guardian*, April 15, 2014. https://www.theguardian.com /world/2014/apr/15/india-recognises -transgender-people-third-gender.

Beresford, Meka. "Transgender Day of Remembrance Held Today to Remember Those Killed by Transphobic Violence." Pink News, November 20, 2016. http://www.pinknews .co.uk/2016/11/20/people-come-together -in-the-thousands-for-transgender-day-of -remembrance.

Bray, Marianne. "A Eunuch's Tale from the Slums: A Glimpse into a Secretive World Reveals a Hard Life." CNN, October 7, 2005. http://edition.cnn .com/2005/WORLD/asiapcf/09/07/india.eye .eunuch.

Fiaz, Faizan. "Officially Recognized but Publicly Shamed: Transgender Life in Pakistan." Vice News, November 26, 2015. https://news.vice .com/article/officially-recognized-but-publicly -shamed-transgender-life-in-pakistan.

Huffington Post. "The Beautiful Way Hawaiian

Culture Embraces a Particular Kind of Transgender Identity." March 28, 2015. http://www.huffingtonpost.com/2015/04/28/hawaiian-culture-transgender_n_7158130.html.

Joyce, Rosemary A. *Ancient Bodies, Ancient Lives*. New York, NY: Thames & Hudson, 2008.

Kulick, Don. *Travesti: Sex, Gender, and Culture Among Brazilian Transgendered Prostitutes*. Chicago, IL: University of Chicago Press, 2009.

Letman, Jon. "'Mahu' Demonstrate Hawaii's Shifting Attitudes Toward LGBT Life." Al Jazeera America, January 9, 2016. http://america.aljazeera.com/articles/2016/1/9/mahu-hawaii-gender-LGBT-acceptance.html.

Nanda, Serena. *Gender Diversity Crosscultural Variations*. 2nd ed. Long Grove, IN: Waveland Press, 2014.

Roscoe, Will. *Changing Ones: Third and Fourth Genders in Native North America*. New York, NY: Palgrave Macmillan, 2000.

Snow, Jade. "What Native Hawaiian Culture Can Teach Us About Gender Identity." *Yes! Magazine*, July 27, 2015. http://www.yesmagazine.org/issues/make-it-right/what-native-hawaiian-culture-can-teach-us-about-gender-identity.

Stryker, Susan. *Transgender History*. Berkley, CA: Seal Press, 2008.

Townsen, Meagan. "Timeline: A Look Back at the History of Transgender Visibility." GLAAD, November 19, 2012. http://www.glaad.org/blog/timeline-look-back-history-transgender-visibility.

INDEX

A

AIDS Coalition to Unleash
  Power (ACT UP), 56
alyha ceremony, 30
antidiscrimination laws, 18, 90

B

bade, 26
Bahuchara Mata, 73, 76, 77
Batgirl, 88
bathroom bills, 90
Benjamin, Harry, 53
berdache, 23–25
Berlin, Germany, 47, 50, 57
binary thinking, explanation, 6
Blackstone, Elliot, 65–67
Bougainville, Louis-Antoine
  de, 34
Brazil, gender roles in, 10–11
Brazilian travestis
  and Brazilian culture,
    10–13, 16–18, 20
  contradictions of carnival,
    18–20
  violence toward, 16–18

C

Central City Anti-Poverty
  Program, 65
Christianity and Catholicism,
  18, 19, 29, 31, 33, 44,
  46, 59

cisgender, explanation of, 8
Close, Roberta, 14–16
clothing/dress, 7, 21, 25,
  26, 29, 30, 39, 52, 59,
  63, 64, 67–68, 73, 74,
  76, 77, 89, 94
Compton's Cafeteria riot,
  64, 65
concentration camps,
  55–56, 57
conversion therapy, 94
Cox, Laverne, 83–85

D

Dallas Buyers Club, 85
Danish Girl, The, 85
DeLarverie, Storme, 70
*Diagnostic and Statistical
  Manual of Mental
  Disorders II* (*DSM*), 94
dos Santos, Dandara, 18

E

Einstein, Albert, 47
Elbe, Lili, 50–52, 60
Ergestrassse, Louise, 65
eunuchs, 45, 77

F

fakaleiti, 39, 43
Foundation for Personality
  Expression, 63

U

V

W

Y

ABOUT THE AUTHOR

Rita Santos has written three books for children and young adults and edited many books for adults. She earned a masters of science in publishing from Pace University. When she's not writing or editing, she loves traveling. Her greatest adventure so far was meeting sloths at the Sloth Sanctuary in Costa Rica. She is also a debt activist who advocates for the rights of student and medical debtors. Santos and her family live in New York City. They hope to adopt several cats in the near future.

PHOTO CREDITS